What Our Readers Have Said...

"The Pinpoint Training Series delivers information that could be used in a lot different areas."

•

"Applicable and valid. The information is good."

•

"I like this because I can take them with me to read at a convenient time. I feel the little time I have to spend in the office is best use on activities that directly relate to revenue opportunities. I like the short amount of time it takes to keep up with these."

•

"I just read each book, and then file it for future reference."

•

"My thought is that the real value of these books comes into effect when doing the action plans."

•

"The challenge when I think a specific topic does not apply is to find a way to make it apply."

•

"Easy to use, understand, and reference if needed."

•

"Good layout and to the point."

•

"I think a lot of the recommendations in these books are very useful, and can be applicable to everyday situations. If nothing else, it's a good reference guide to fall back upon if a situation arises in the future."

•

"These books are relevant to today's work environment and the ongoing change in the way we manage our workforce."

•

"These books will pay for the time that I am investing. There are numerous good ideas that will streamline what I do and how I do it."

•

"All and all I think the Pinpoint series is a good program. I know other people I would love to have something like this. I think a lot of the suggestions are very useful, and can be applicable to everyday situations. If nothing else it's a good reference guide to fall back upon if a situation arises in the future."

•

"These books reinforce many concepts that I have learned through seminars, schooling and other programs. For myself, it serves as a constant learning tool that keeps me on top of the issues that many of us encounter every day."

•

"All in all, I think you have good training books. It helps everyone to review these materials, it serves as a good reminder to us on how to conduct ourselves."

•

"The information is valuable in these books."

•

"Good thoughts and ideas."

•

"I believe these books would be valuable to all employees."

•

Motivating Employees

Pinpoint Management Skill Development Training Series

TIMOTHY F. BEDNARZ

MAJORIUM
BUSINESS PRESS

Pinpoint Management Skill Development Training Series
"Motivating Employees"
Timothy F. Bednarz

Graphic design: Monika Pawlak

Majorium Business Press
2025 Main Street
Stevens Point, WI 54481
715.342.1018 • 800.654.4935

ISBN 978-1-882181-52-0

Printed in the United States of America

Introduction

The Pinpoint Management Skill Development Training Series is designed for targeted training and education regarding increased improvement in a specific skill or competency.

Each book within this series is designed to be easy to use, understand and apply to your job. It can be used as a basis for training individuals, as a discussion guide or as a personal training tool.

Each chapter within this book discusses a specific concept. When you have completed all eight chapters you should have a 360° perspective of the topic.

Additionally, each chapter is divided into specific sections:

- The first section provides you with an overview of the topic
- The Implications section discusses why the concept is important, and why it is important to learn and apply.
- The Strategies, Tips & Techniques to Apply section teaches how to use and apply the particular concept to your work.
- The Points to Ponder section gives you something to think about or to be discussed with a group setting. These are questions not meant to be immediately answered, but to be pondered over time.
- The Training Activity section provides you with the tools to transfer what you have learned to your job. It is designed to help create an action plan to effectively apply the concept.

Each of the topics in this series is time-tested and proven in the marketplace. They have been used by thousands of employees as training tools. Many of the users have commented that what made these books valuable, was the ability to refer to them when a problem surfaced. They indicated that they remembered reading about the exact problem. They referred back to these books and found an appropriate solution.

You will find them equally valuable as a resource in your professional development library.

Table of Contents

LEARNING OBJECTIVES:

- The importance of motivation.
- To take the role of cheerleader for their team.
- To motivate and retain their employees.
- To build self-esteem in their team.

1

The Manager as Cheerleader

At a sporting event, cheerleaders are present for the single purpose of providing support for their team. The same applies to the manager in the workplace. Once plans and programs are in place it becomes the responsibility of the manager to provide the support their employees need to achieve maximum results.

IMPLICATIONS – WHAT THIS MEANS TO YOU

The nature of most positions assumes that employees are self-managing and self-directing in the majority of their activities. The traditional role of the manager was to control and direct the employees they supervised. Effective managers now support and motivate their employees by streamlining policies and procedures and by removing internal barriers to their productivity.

Managers must understand that by removing internal barriers and streamlining procedures they make the employee's job easier, allowing each one to focus on more productive tasks rather than diverting their energy elsewhere. In this manner, the role of the manager is to keep their employees on track and motivated to reach their peak performance.

STRATEGIES, TIPS & TECHNIQUES TO APPLY

The role of the manager is to remove the roadblocks their employees encounter in order to enhance their productivity. Effective managers understand it is their primary responsibility to produce results and not just control and direct. Efficiency and productivity are the means to achieving results, and managers need to make attaining them as easy as possible. This is achieved by providing the following:

Attainable Goals

One of the primary responsibilities of a manager is to ensure that their employees have realistic and attainable goals. This does not necessarily mean that goals are easy; rather, they should always stretch the employee's ability to grow. However, unrealistic and overwhelming goals and objectives are counterproductive because they frustrate and ultimately de-motivate the employee.

Employees are responsible for developing their own work-related goals. In many cases they are accepted with little or no scrutiny. Managers should invest the time and resources to have a frank discussion with all individuals concerning their objectives. For example, IBM built their success by ensuring that their employees had a series of smaller, attainable goals. When those were achieved, employees' successes were celebrated.

Managers should likewise require that their own employees develop a series of smaller plans for the quarter, month, week and day, all linked to the accomplishment of larger goals. In this manner, managers help their employees stay focused on activities that keep them moving forward toward the accomplishment of their objectives.

Without this critical guidance and direction, all unit or department activities for the year may prove wasteful and meaningless. When realistic and attainable plans are in place, the role of the manager is to support their employees' activities and keep them on track and focused on the results they need to achieve.

Adequate Support

Employees must be provided the necessary tools and resources to achieve the desired results. A lack of adequate support for an employee sends a mixed message and hurts motivation. During the heat of daily activities, employees need timely information, data and support in order to keep moving forward.

When companies fail employees at these critical junctures, they are communicating their lack of concern for their efforts. This often undermines the investment in time and resources made by the worker. If it costs him or her meeting a particular target or goal, motivation to work hard toward the next objective is eliminated. It is replaced with an "If they don't care, why should I?" attitude. Once this attitude takes hold it is difficult to reverse.

Realistic Reports and Policies

Employees can be burdened with scheduled reports that are generated more out of tradition than need. Aside from the expense and resource utilization reports required as management tools, managers should only request the information they need to monitor the success of the employee's plan. Beyond that, many reports can duplicate information and may be throwbacks to outdated pre-computer days.

With the advent of computers and business management software, yesterday's report can easily be transformed into an action plan. This process provides both the manager and employee with an informational tool that directs and informs.

Managers need quality information to monitor their employees' activities, which can be obtained through a performance metrics system that reports key numbers to reflect the employee's activities. Typically, such metrics accurately report the progress of activities within the employee's pipeline.

Effective Skills Development

Managers must ensure that their employees continually polish their skills, which requires providing quality training while monitoring an individual employee's performance to observe what skills are in need of refinement. When necessary, additional training and coaching may be required. Training should not be considered merely as a reward, but as a requirement if employees are to grow in their profession.

POINTS TO PONDER — SOMETHING TO THINK ABOUT

1. Do you feel that you are providing the needed amount of support for your employees to be successful?
2. What additional things can you do to enhance employee efforts?

TRAINING ACTIVITY — APPLICATION & ACTION PLAN

Examine the areas discussed above to determine how you can streamline certain procedures in order to provide better support for your employees:

- Attainable Goals
- Adequate Support
- Realistic Reports and Policies
- Effective Skills Development

2

The Basis of Motivation

All employees are unique in what motivates them to perform to their capacity and excel in their profession. Most will do what is expected of them, but the motivated employee will go to great lengths to exceed expectations. The key is for managers to discover what truly drives their people. Once their motivation is understood, leaders have the power to get the most out of their employees.

IMPLICATIONS – WHAT THIS MEANS TO YOU

Managers often feel there is no need to motivate their employees as long as the pay is adequate. Yet research has demonstrated that the majority of personal motivation is based upon a host of other significant factors such as achievement, recognition, responsibility, personal growth, and advancement. Compensation is certainly a motivating factor, but it is often linked to these more prime motivators. A poorly designed compensation plan will cause employees to feel unappreciated and not be reflective of their personal achievements. Consequently, many employees link their compensation to their perception of how they are recognized within the organization.

Managers must understand that it is within their power and control to motivate each member of their team to excel.

STRATEGIES, TIPS & TECHNIQUES TO APPLY

Managers who wish to maximize their employees' performance use specific motivators to create an environment in which individuals feel valued for their contributions to the company, know their efforts are appreciated and supported by the organization, and have the desire to achieve higher levels of personal performance. These results can be achieved by nurturing an atmosphere that includes the following elements:

Interest

Managers must take a genuine personal interest in each employee. Although significant, this means going beyond his or her life outside of work. The main areas in which to devote individual attention are in mentoring and nurturing a personal and professional growth as well as in understanding what motivates them. When managers demonstrate an interest in their employees, they are giving and sharing their time, lives and expertise with their employees.

Confidence

Managers who wish to motivate their employees must develop confidence in their abilities. This means allowing employees to experiment with new ideas and techniques while understanding that, as people grow through their experiences, many lessons are best learned through personal mistakes and failure.

Managers must also have the confidence that their employees can develop realistic and attainable plans and allow them to work those plans without interference or micromanagement. Individuals who know they have the liberty to perform their jobs without fear of retribution if they falter are more motivated and empowered to stretch the limits of their capabilities.

Challenge

Employees must be challenged to stretch their personal and professional limits. This includes personal and professional development in areas of vocational knowledge, skills and expertise.

Pride

Managers must maintain a sense of pride in their team, their company and the products they sell. Employees must continually sell themselves on the value of the company and its products or services. If employees aren't sold, they will have difficulty convincing others of the company's worth. Additionally, as people need a spark to overcome daily stress and adversity, managers must build and nurture a passion in their employees to achieve and succeed.

Bonding

Managers must establish a sense of fellowship between the individual members of their workplace, which thereby creates comradery and emotional support. Successfully done, this builds a strong team atmosphere and healthy sense of friendly competition that is beneficial to the organization.

Reward and Recognition

Managers should use fair and consistent standards with which to measure performance and base rewards and recognition. Employees should be evaluated against their own performance, and, for best impact, appropriate recognition should be given immediately.

Appreciation

Beyond tangible rewards and recognition, managers must demonstrate their personal appreciation for the efforts and contributions made by their individual employees. They should also avoid taking the top performers on their team for granted. Because these individuals need little attention or direction, they are often overlooked as managers invest more time with more inexperienced or problematic employees. To stretch their personal abilities, the best of the group also need ongoing recognition, appreciation and encouragement.

POINTS TO PONDER – SOMETHING TO THINK ABOUT

1. Which positive motivators do you employ to encourage and push your employees?
2. Have you found a single motivator that is especially effective for each employee?

TRAINING ACTIVITY – APPLICATION & ACTION PLAN

Reviewing the seven motivators listed below, identify specific ways to implement each of them with your employees. If you are already using some of them, identify ways to make improvements to increase their effectiveness.

- Interest
- Confidence
- Challenge
- Pride
- Bonding
- Reward
- Appreciation

3

Techniques to Motivate Teams and Work Groups

If managers want to truly motivate their employees, they must review the broader combination of factors that can impact performance. These factors go beyond the primary issue of money, rewards and recognition.

IMPLICATIONS – WHAT THIS MEANS TO YOU

Effective motivational techniques require managers to look beyond the issue of compensation or commission and to view all of the factors that can affect the individual employee's performance.

It is important to understand that people are motivated by a number of different factors. A failure to grasp the larger situation can result in hidden factors that serve to undermine the motivation of employees rather than urge them to achieve to their maximum levels of performance.

STRATEGIES, TIPS & TECHNIQUES TO APPLY

There are a number of aspects that managers need to consider when developing a program that maintains peak motivation levels in the workplace. These include:

Reward and Recognition

Reward and recognition are two of the primary issues that arise when motivation is discussed. Managers must discover what motivates employees to achieve their goals and objectives and then confer rewards for superior performance. There are a number of companies that provide incentive programs. Managers need to determine what will best drive employee performance and then make these types of rewards available.

How to recognize employees' achievements can be a more complex issue. The best approach is to query individual employees to determine how to recognize their superior performance, with what frequency and how publicly. The manager who takes the time and effort to discover these answers can make the difference between fostering a quality workforce and losing it.

Effective Use

Nothing can de-motivate an individual employee more than having their skills underutilized or having to be placed into a position where he or she feels ineffective or weak.

Every employee has his or her own particular strengths. The astute manager knows how to best position each employee for success and places them on teams or in specific situations that best leverage their particular strengths.

Collaboration

Employees can be motivated when they are allowed to collaborate with others to implement new ideas, concepts and approaches in order to increase revenue or overall efficiency. In other circumstances, employees can collaborate with others on teams to enhance working relationships within the company.

Collaboration allows employees to stretch their abilities and contribute their skills on a broader scale than normal. However, managers must ensure that all employees in collaborative efforts are cooperating with each other. Otherwise, motivated employees can begin to lose their drive and fail to produce the work expected of them.

Effective Training

In many companies, training is given a cursory nod. However, employees are certainly motivated and receptive to effective training that provides them with new skills, approaches and techniques, which in turn give them the competitive edge they need for continued success. Managers that provide a continuous flow of effective training thus continue to motivate their teams.

Cooperation

One of the areas stymieing many employees is the lack of communication between sales, production and other critical support areas. When employees develop and maintain open communication with these areas, they are better and more quickly able to respond to daily problems and concerns.

Cooperation goes beyond good communication. The ability to work directly with critical departments to provide superior products and services improves overall effectiveness and professionalism.

Support

If employees can completely rely on their manager to support their efforts, then they will be motivated to maximize their performance.

Managers who are open and available to individual members of their team and are willing to assist each one independently—no matter what the problem—find that they build a loyal and motivated workforce.

When managers are inconsistent or judgmental, they undermine this loyalty and remove the personal motivation and desire for employees to excel.

Coaching and Encouragement

Managers build their employees' motivation through personal encouragement and by helping them hone and polish their skills. This also means working with poorly performing individuals and, if their performance fails to improve, removing them before they have a negative effect on the general workplace.

POINTS TO PONDER – SOMETHING TO THINK ABOUT

1. Have you considered the list of factors in this lesson and how they impact your employees' motivation levels?
2. How do you determine which factors effect and influence positive employee performance?

TRAINING ACTIVITY – APPLICATION & ACTION PLAN

Using the list of factors below, review how each can be used to positively impact the performance of your employees.

- Rewards & Recognition
- Effective Use of Skills and Abilities
- Collaboration
- Effective Training
- Cooperation
- Support
- Coaching & Encouragement

4

Motivation Is More Than Money

When the topic of workplace motivation arises, the two primary issues managers focus on are rewards and recognition. This recognition often takes the form of compensation, but can also be manifested as accurate and timely feedback that acknowledges both positive and negative performance.

IMPLICATIONS — WHAT THIS MEANS TO YOU

Many managers have focused their motivational efforts on the financial compensation an employee receives for their efforts. However, many have failed to understand the impact that clearly defined tasks and fast and accurate feedback have on their workforce. Consequently, they fail to ensure that both positive and negative feedback provided to their employees is directly related to their performance.

Aside from financial and budgetary means, it is important for managers to understand that they can increase overall performance through effective motivational techniques that increase employee

STRATEGIES, TIPS & TECHNIQUES TO APPLY

Harvard Business School conducted a number of employee surveys in a variety of industries. The hypothesis was that the employees who were paid the highest salaries and who had the appropriate personality traits, including drive and confidence, would be the best performers.

This hypothesis was soon discovered to be faulty. The actual top performing employees were defined not only by money, but by the following three factors:

Personal Impact – The top performers had the personality to bring about results through their own efforts. Each was able to accomplish their goals through their individual drive.

Fast Feedback – The top performers knew quickly whether or not their efforts worked. The low motivation employees were unsure of their results and unable to gauge their performance.

Accurate Feedback – The top performers received truthful feedback that accurately reflected their personal impact on results. They knew exactly where they stood and received credit when it was due. The low motivation employees were neither recognized for their good work nor penalized for poor performance. The challenge was thus removed from their jobs, as it was of no consequence whether they excelled or failed.

The results of the Harvard Business School study reveal that the nature of the task and feedback ultimately determine the employee's motivation. The study indicated that these two factors are more important motivators than compensation.

There are several steps a manager can take to apply this information to their workplace:

- Ensure tasks assigned to employees are clear. The employees should know exactly what is expected of them. These expectations are inherently motivating.
- Make the connection between the employee's individual performance and the end result obvious.
- Teach employees to evaluate their own work. Detail the critical factors of success and provide them with an evaluation form to use. Make it clear that employees are responsible for their own assessment, and that they can perform the evaluation as frequently as they find it necessary.
- When providing feedback, managers should ask, rather than tell, em-

ployees what happened in specific situations, especially if the manager was not an eyewitness. This process is important since customer feedback is often perceived to be inaccurate. Basing feedback on inaccurate information often results in resentment.

- Educate employees regarding how to use feedback. If employees fail to understand how feedback relates to their performance, there is no context in which to place it in, and it becomes meaningless.

POINTS TO PONDER – SOMETHING TO THINK ABOUT

1. Have you ever used "task clarity" to motivate your employees?
2. Do you feel that instant and accurate feedback has a motivating effect on your employees?

TRAINING ACTIVITY – APPLICATION & ACTION PLAN

Develop a self-evaluation form for your employees to use.

1. Identify key factors and functions that should be evaluated.
2. Determine whether any other elements should be incorporated.
3. Develop a simple ranking system (e.g. a scale of 1-10).
4. Print out a form for their personal use.
5. Duplicate, distribute and educate employees in how to use it.

5

Retaining Employees

Retaining quality employees is one of the most significant challenges managers face. Even the decision to terminate a marginal performer must be reviewed in light of the costs and benefits associated with recruiting and training a replacement.

IMPLICATIONS – WHAT THIS MEANS TO YOU

Retention of quality employees should be a top priority for all managers. While it may be desirable to remove a marginal performer, managers need to consider alternatives to recruiting, hiring and training a new employee. It is often less expensive to invest the time and effort to coach and mentor a marginal performer than it is to recruit and train a new employee. It is important for managers to realize that beyond the costs associated with recruiting, hiring and training a new employee, one must consider the time and interruption associated with accomplishing these tasks.

STRATEGIES, TIPS & TECHNIQUES TO APPLY

There are a number of ways that managers can retain quality employees, including:

Model Behavior

The individual manager can have either a positive or negative impact on their employees through their management style, personal ethics and consistency. A good manager builds personal loyalty among their employees and fosters a desire in each to succeed and excel. Conversely, a poor manager undermines and de-motivates his or her employees, causing a loss of their best performers.

Accept the Learning Process

The nature of daily business means that employees are constantly faced with the prospect of stress and failure. The learning process can be merciless in revealing mistakes on the part of the employee and manager.

Managers must recognize mistakes and realize that they act as an aid in increasing personal performance and improvement.

Boost Self-Esteem

Employees need to continually have their self-esteem buoyed in the face of daily pressures and inevitable mistakes. It is only natural for many to have battered and bruised egos. Managers need to help their people feel good about themselves. When employees do something exceptional, managers need to take the time to recognize it.

Create a Learning Environment

In order to achieve a competitive edge, employees need a continuous flow of information, tactics and techniques to help hone their skills. Employees must be given the opportunities and incentives to invest in their own professional development.

Effective Communication

The consistent flow of timely information is essential for employees. Managers should use all available methods, including email, faxes, meetings, and intranet to keep employees informed of company goals, objectives and changing tactics and strategies.

Recognize Achievement

Managers must understand that personal recognition for a job well done needs to be emphasized. Such recognition, linked with adequate income and personal security, is generally the most important to employees.

Managers should further be aware of the career goals of their individual employees and take action to assure that they achieve them. When employees demonstrate superior performance, managers must ensure their performance is brought to the attention of the company so that they can be given recognition and promotion.

Attractive Work Environment

Managers should ensure that employees have a safe and attractive working environment. Such an environment is a reflection of the business.

Maintain Flexibility

Managers must retain flexibility within the job. They must understand that employees have lives outside of work and obligations to their families, including mortgages, tuition and medical expenses. Consideration should be given to family matters, personal interests and aspirations. Benefits in specific areas allow employees to concentrate on their job. It is important that managers recognize their employees need to have realistic time schedules that allow them to spend time outside of work, and that small allowances for such personal pursuits will often yield large returns in productivity.

POINTS TO PONDER — SOMETHING TO THINK ABOUT

1. How successful are you in retaining your better employees? To what do you attribute your success (or lack thereof)?
2. What specific steps do you take to convert employees into quality performers?

TRAINING ACTIVITY — APPLICATION & ACTION PLAN

1. Review the factors below that tend to impact the retention of employees inside your company.
2. Determine if there are any areas that need improvement.
3. Specifically identify what can be done to improve each of them.
    - Modeling Behavior
    - Accepting the Learning Process
    - Boosting Self-Esteem
    - Creating a Learning Environment
    - Communicating Effectively
    - Recognizing Achievement
    - Developing an Attractive Work Environment
    - Maintaining Flexibility

6

Expectations Are Everything

During the 1930s researchers from Harvard University conducted productivity studies at Western Electric's Hawthorne facility that demonstrated how management attention generates immediate productivity increases. However sustained, long-term productivity is facilitated when management communicates the consistent message that employees will perform to the expectations of established standards.

IMPLICATIONS – WHAT THIS MEANS TO YOU

More than 300 additional studies support the fact that an employee's achievement goes beyond their individual personal ability and mirrors their manager's expectations. These findings indicate that employees perform in accordance with what is expected of them, even above their own beliefs in their abilities. This fact can play a significant role when it comes to individual performance.

It is important for managers to understand that if they openly demonstrate they believe an employee to be competent and worthwhile, then he or she is likely to be more effective and perceive their job to be more rewarding. Managers reinforce this concept when they encourage and are responsive to their employees, provide them more challenging assignments, and offer additional assistance and support whenever needed.

STRATEGIES, TIPS & TECHNIQUES TO APPLY

The phenomenon commonly referred to as the Pygmalion Effect stresses that achievement mirrors expectations more than individual ability. An individual's performance is affected by his or her self-image. This concept sets the boundaries of individual accomplishment. Its main principle supports the belief that employees can work up to and beyond their own perceived abilities by rising to meet the expectations managers have of them.

Managers have the ability to alter overall performance through expanding their employees' self-confidence and by building their self-esteem. These actions impact performance by expanding individual personal perceptions of what one can accomplish.

The nature of business means employees must deal with daily stress and inevitable missteps and failures that impact their self-esteem and confidence. Managers can positively support their employees by keeping the Pygmalion Effect in mind. They can build expectations that employees will readily overcome any setbacks and continue to work toward success.

A manager's attitude toward their employees also directly affects their performance. They are often astonished to discover that when employees are given a chance to prove themselves, they display more talent and ability than the manager initially imagined.

The second aspect of increasing productivity is the level of attention provided by managers. Attitudes, expectations and attention establish what gets done and how. The Hawthorne studies show that the time and attention invested by management is directly proportional to results. In most organizations time is the scarcest of available resources. Employees understand that when a manager is visible to them, he or she is investing a valuable personal resource in their performance. Consequently, a visible manager is an effective one.

When most people think about leadership, they perceive it to be found only at the top levels of an organization. However, in reality, effective leadership takes place on a one-to-one basis. Managers work directly with each of their employees to enhance their capabilities and personal commitment to achieve positive results. The power of a single manager's attitude, expectations and attention can impact productivity and positive results more radically than anything else.

Organizational changes actually occur on individual levels. Good managers understand that success occurs slowly but consistently, one small change at a time. While each single change may not appear meaningful unto itself, when measured across time and the entire workplace, the impact is enormous.

When managers positively impact their employees' performance to increase their productivity step-by-step, they begin to contribute consistently and successfully toward the achievement of the organization's goals. Each small success builds ongoing commitment. Overall change occurs because everyone has a chance to commit and contribute to it. Progress is the result of many things being done differently—not major management decisions.

POINTS TO PONDER — SOMETHING TO THINK ABOUT

1. Have you ever personally mentored an employee to build his or her expectations? What resulted?
2. What are your personal expectations of the employees you manage?

TRAINING ACTIVITY — APPLICATION & ACTION PLAN

1. Make a list of the people who have had a powerful impact and influence on your life.
2. Identify the specific factors that made them effective as coaches and mentors.
3. Determine what traits, attitudes and beliefs they all had in common that created the positive impact on your life and career.

7

The Tangible Aspects of Motivation

In some companies, under the premise that they will be perceived more meaningful, rewards and recognitions are given so infrequently as to in fact be meaningless. In order to be effective in generating long-term, concrete results, such rewards, recognitions and motivation must be given liberally, frequently and publicly. They should be fun, uplifting and encourage all members of the workplace.

IMPLICATIONS – WHAT THIS MEANS TO YOU

A critical aspect of leadership is the manager's role as cheerleader. Leaders need to keep their employees motivated and emotionally prepared to do business in a marketplace fraught with intense competition, rejection and failure.

There are both tangible and intangible aspects of motivation. The intangible aspects of encouraging words and pats on the back, although not insignificant, can be quickly forgotten, while the tangible aspects are visible and durable.

Napoleon discovered long ago that men would walk into combat and perform daring feats for a piece of ribbon and scrap of metal. Managers should learn from this lesson: it's not the value of a reward or recognition, but what that reward stands for. People will move mountains for the right reward.

STRATEGIES, TIPS & TECHNIQUES TO APPLY

The late Curtis Carlson, founder of Radisson Hotels, T.G.I. Friday's, Carlson Wagonlit Travel and a host of other hospitality companies, was a master motivator. During an interview on CNN's *Pinnacle* years ago, he discussed the tangible aspects of motivation.

Carlson started his career as an employee for S&H Green Stamps, a company that used stamps as a retail incentive tool. In his capacity as an employee, Carlson achieved a specific sales goal and was awarded an engraved watch. He observed that everywhere he went his wife made him take off his self-described $20 watch so that she could display it to their friends. He took this lesson with him in his rise to the top of corporate America.

The lesson Carlson learned was the tangible value of motivation. He said that one could give an employee a $20 bonus on Friday, and by Monday it was spent and forgotten. But if one gave them a framed certificate or some other tangible form of recognition, it was there as a constant reminder of their accomplishments.

A very visible example of his practice is seen at T.G.I. Friday's. A tradition in the company is for the employees to sport colorful vests full of motivational pins from all of the restaurants they've worked at. Carlson was a skillful practitioner of tangible motivation: he knew the public display of recognition and accomplishment had an enduring effect long after the individual was honored.

Managers can take a page from the Carlson book and create their own tangible motivation program. As Carlson learned, the action doesn't have to be expensive, only tangible, frequent, visible and durable.

People love to be recognized and honored. Most have a wall of items at home or in the office to show the world what they've achieved and accomplished. They want others to recognize that they have made a difference.

Many managers will use monetary awards or gifts as incentives—some to a great degree, such as Mary Kay Cosmetics, who awards their top employees pink Cadillacs. As Carlson learned, money or a disposable gift such as food, a car wash or a trip is quickly forgotten. Instead managers should consider ideas like certificates, pins, coffee cups and other items that will be used and remain visible in the workplace as motivational tools. Some organizations have used items such as gold plated spark plugs as symbols of accomplishment.

Another key to tangible motivation is frequency. Carlson learned that to be effective, recognition must be as frequent and public as possible. Tom Peters discussed this concept in his book, *Catching Someone Doing Something Right.* Too often, managers only identify the negative aspects of their employees' performance. Peters talks about turning this concept around by looking for and immediately recognizing the positives.

The final aspect of motivation is public recognition, which builds self-confidence and self-esteem while fostering team spirit and a strong sense of comradery.

There are many sides and aspects to motivation, but the fun and frivolous aspects of public and tangible motivation do work. Managers will be amazed at the amount of effort their employees will expend to earn a piece of paper or inexpensive knick-knack.

POINTS TO PONDER — SOMETHING TO THINK ABOUT

1. What is the single reward, recognition or honor in your career that you remember most? Why?
2. Conversely, what was a recognition you received, but quickly forgot about? Why?

TRAINING ACTIVITY — APPLICATION & ACTION PLAN

1. Be creative. Develop a tangible motivational tradition for your employees. Remember, it is not the value of the motivational tool selected, but the fact that it's concrete, frequent, durable and visible.
2. Consider an item such as a funny type of pen, poster or some other simple

object. Let it become a traditional symbol of accomplishment.

3. Create a reward system around it.

8

Critical Skills that Determine Positive Self-Development

The complexion of management is changing. In a volatile business environment, the skills required of managers in the past have become antiquated and outmoded. Managers are required to either adapt or lose their professional effectiveness. There are a number of critical skills that they are required to master if they wish to remain relevant for their company.

IMPLICATIONS – WHAT THIS MEANS TO YOU

Most managers would like to maintain the status quo. It is easy to be resistant to change and its impact on the business environment; in fact, many managers are doing just that, hoping that conditions will revert to the way they were in the past. Such wishful thinking has no basis in fact, but does have numerous adverse consequences.

It is important for managers to understand that things will never be the same and that the impact of change is a reality they must comprehend and deal with. They must adapt their thinking to continually evolve with changes in the global marketplace. New skills are required of managers to integrate these alterations into their business and adapt to future changes.

STRATEGIES, TIPS & TECHNIQUES TO APPLY

Managers must understand that there are a number of skills they must develop that constitute enhanced self-improvement and professional development. These skills are in fact strongly linked to a manager's job performance. They must foster their professional ability to:

Think Outside the Box

A manager's personal thinking is often shaped by the events and circumstances he or she has experienced. Over time, they have the tendency to become myopic and completely focused on the day-to-day activities of the company. Therefore, they develop a biased perspective that may not reflect a larger reality.

Change demands that managers climb outside of their own perspective to develop a fresh view of both their company and the reality of the business environment. This process often results in a paradigm shift in thinking that impacts future business practices and methods. Managers are compelled to recognize the dynamic reality of the business environment and how change is affecting their business.

Change the Culture

Linked with a shift in thinking is the required adaptation in the corporate culture that is necessitated by change. Managers often have difficulty dealing with the concept of changing the culture around them, mostly out of fear of the personal consequences that come with challenging conventional wisdom. Many do not appreciate the need to evolve as leaders—beyond managers who only supervise and direct—and the subsequent risk they take on by not assuming the leadership role required to help effect the culture change. While they might keep the peace for the time being, the consequences of their failure to adapt will more often than not catch up with them in the future.

Monitor the Pulse of the Business

The professional development of managers demands that they delegate more of their daily tactical activities and responsibilities to individual employees.

While this pushes decision making down to the front lines of the business where it has the most impact, it does not mean the manager should ignore what is happening within his or her unit. Rather, they should use performance metrics to daily monitor the pulse of what is actually happening with their people. While delegating their micromanagement activities, it is important to maintain an active presence with their team, which allows them to actively interact with any individual employee when required.

Act Quickly

As managers create a leadership style, they also must incorporate the ability to act quickly and decisively. In a business environment of rapid change, hesitancy is not a desirable trait in managers, especially in an environment where a failure to act can easily create an opening.

Keep It Simple

While many managers have developed a notion that the more complicated the plan or goal the better, the successful manager understands the need to keep things simple and straightforward, and to stress execution.

Complicated plans and solutions demand complicated and costly support systems. Such systems are also prone to human error and increase the risk of failure. Conversely, simple plans are typically less expensive, not nearly as subject to human error, and are easier to execute and implement.

Develop Self-Confidence

Managers who desire to develop their professional skills must cultivate a sense of confidence in their own decisions. Many fall into the trap of constantly second-guessing themselves, which results in hesitancy and loss of confidence in their professional abilities. It is a far more desirable managerial trait to act quickly and decisively, and then make any needed modifications later as additional data and results become available.

POINTS TO PONDER – SOMETHING TO THINK ABOUT

1. How proactive are you in developing necessary leadership skills?
2. What prevents you from personally developing newly required skills?

TRAINING ACTIVITY – APPLICATION & ACTION PLAN

1. List the following skills on a sheet of paper. Identify which specific ones you are personally proficient at.
    - Thinking outside the box
    - Changing the culture
    - Keeping a pulse on the workplace
    - Acting quickly
    - Keeping it simple
    - Developing self-confidence
2. Identify particular areas of weakness that appear to require improvement.
3. Based upon your self-assessment, create a program to strengthen certain necessary skills.

About the Author

Timothy F. Bednarz, Ph.D. is CEO of the American Management Development Group, Inc. For over 20 years he has researched, designed and authored hundreds of learning and development programs used by Fortune 1000 companies.

He is also the author of *Great! What Makes Leaders Great. What They Did, How They Did It and What You Can Learn from It* (2011).

Speaking Availability

Timothy F. Bednarz, Ph.D. is available for speaking engagements for your next meeting or association event. He can be contacted at 800-654-4935 or by e-mail at timothy.bednarz@majorium.com.

Bulk Sales

Bulk sales of this book or any other titles available from Majorium Business Press. Inquiries can be directed to sales@majorium.com, or by phone at 800-6654-4935.

Quick Order Form

Fax orders: 715-342-1118. Send this form.

Telephone orders: Call 800-654-4935 toll-free. Have your credit card ready.

Email orders: sales@majorium.com

Postal orders: Majorium Business Press, 2025 Main Street, Stevens Point, WI 54481, USA.

Please send the following books:

____

____

____

____

Please send more FREE information on:

❑Catalog ❑Speaking/Seminars ❑Mailing Lists ❑Consulting

Name: ____________________________________

Address: __________________________________

City: ____________________ State: _____ Zip: _________

Telephone: ________________________________

Email address: _____________________________

Sales tax: Please add 5.5% for products shipped to Wisconsin addresses.

Shipping by air:

United States: $4.00 for first book and $2.00 for each additional product.

International: $9.00 for first book; $5.00 for each additional product (estimate).

Made in United States
Cleveland, OH
05 November 2026

47664317R10026